Greater Th Antigua Guatemala

50 Travel Tips from a Local

Rachael Haylock

Rachael Haylock

Order Information: To order this title please email lbrenenc@gmail.com or visit GreaterThanATourist.com. A bulk discount can be provided.

Cover Template Creator: Lisa Rusczyk Ed. D. using Canva.
Cover Creator: Lisa Rusczyk Ed. D.
Image: https://pixabay.com/en/cross-praise-christian-guatemala-2536818/

Lock Haven, PA
All rights reserved.
ISBN: 9781549680380

>TOURIST

Rachael Haylock

BOOK DESCRIPTION

Are you excited about planning your next trip?

Do you want to try something new?

Would you like some guidance from a local?

If you answered yes to any of these questions, then this Greater Than a Tourist book is for you.

Greater Than a Tourist Antigua Guatemala by Rachael Haylock offers the inside scoop on Antigua. Most travel books tell you how to sightsee. Although there's nothing wrong with that, as a part of the Greater than a Tourist series, this book will give you tips from someone who lives at your next travel destination. In these pages, you'll discover local advice that will help you throughout your trip. Travel like a local. Slow down and get to know the people and the culture of a place. By the time you finish this book, you will be eager and prepared to travel to your next destination.

Rachael Haylock

TABLE OF CONTENTS

10. Learn how to Farm

11. Explore Rooftop Hangouts

12. Find out about Guatemalan History

13. Go to the Art Exhibitions and Museums

14. Watch Interesting Documentaries whilst Eating Bagels

15. Learn what 'Los Tres Tiempos' Actually Means

16. Explore the Market - Food

17. Explore the Market - Artisan

18. Climb Volcano Pacaya

19. Climb Volcano Acatenango

20. Where to Stay

21. Keeping Fit

22. Where to Find the Best Coffee

23. Getting Out of Antigua

24. Where to Shop

25. Drink at the Best Bars

26. Where to Eat

27. Take a Walk Through Parque Central

28. Discover the Churches

29. Hike up to Cerro de la Cruz

Rachael Haylock

> TOURIST

Our Story

Notes

DEDICATION

This book is dedicated to a special man I met in the cobblestone streets and volcanic skylines of Antigua and who introduced me to the magic of Guatemala.

Rachael Haylock

ABOUT THE AUTHOR

Rachael is a writer and yoga teacher who currently lives in London. She loves to travel, ultimately to experience and share her life in as many ways as possible. She trained as a dancer, and though this is not her profession, she lives by the motto 'dance as many days as possible' and uses dance as a way to immerse herself into a new culture.

Rachael was born in London and made Antigua her home for three months whilst traveling in Guatemala. She is now in a relationship with a local from Guatemala City and regularly goes back to visit the country, making plans to eventually settle there full time. The following are tips she found helped her the most whilst she adjusted to life in Antigua - or as she calls it - The Cobblestone Jungle.

Rachael Haylock

HOW TO USE THIS BOOK

The Greater Than a Tourist book series was written by someone who has lived in an area for over three months. The goal of this book is to help travelers either dream or experience different locations by providing opinions from a local. The author has made suggestions based on their own experiences. Please do your own research before traveling to the area in case the suggested places are unavailable.

Rachael Haylock

FROM THE PUBLISHER

Traveling can be one of the most important parts of a person's life. The anticipation and memories that you have are some of the best. As a publisher of the Greater Than a Tourist book series, as well as the popular 50 Things to Know book series, we strive to help you learn about new places, spark your imagination, and inspire you. Wherever you are and whatever you do I wish you safe, fun, and inspiring travel.

Lisa Rusczyk Ed. D.

CZYK Publishing

Rachael Haylock

WELCOME TO > TOURIST

Rachael Haylock

INTRODUCTION

As a traveler, the first thing that captivates you about Antigua is how undeniably different it is from the rest of the country. Surrounded by three majestic volcanoes and founded in the mid 1500's by the Spanish conquistadors, Antigua still holds a mystical and colonial feel; it boasts beautiful architecture, elaborate churches and unique ruins, remnants of the Earthquake that destroyed it in the 18th Century

Soaked with history, Antigua now is a hot spot for both tourists, expats and locals alike, and it is distinctive in its richness in both Mayan and Western Cultures. It has restaurants serving food from all over the world, local delicacies and local coffee roasters; roof top bars, salsa clubs and various night-time hangouts. There are spanish schools, guatemalan cooking schools and organic farms where you can learn to grow and cultivate fresh fruits and vegetables.

Whether you want to hustle in the busy markets, learn some Guatemalan culture, or simply relax on the sofas in a breezy rooftop cafe, Antigua definitely has a lot to give.

1. Speak like a Local

Even if you already speak Spanish, you will almost certainly have difficulty understanding the Guatemalan dialect.

Understanding the language is the first step to understanding this beautiful country., and using the local phrases are great conversation starters!

Here are a few useful phrases to give you a head start:

"Que honda maje?" - "Whats up bro"

"Que honda vos?" - Also, "Whats up bro?"

"Puchicas" -To be said when you are surprised by something

"A la gran chucha" - "Oh my god/What the hell/I don't believe it"

"Cerote" - A strange word that you will hear a lot, "Cerote" can be used in familiarity with someone, similar to how we use "dude" or "man", but it can also be used to offend someone. Sometimes it is used to refer to an object, e.g "Hey look over there at that cerote", but can also describe how good or bad someone is at something. A difficult on to get your head around...

"Que chilero" - "That's so cool"

"Que d'huevo" - Also, "Thats so cool"

"A huevo" - "Hell yeah!"

"Dame jalon" - "Give me a ride"

"Va ta bueno" - "Ok whatever"

"Símon" - A one of a kind Spanglish variations, take from the Creole way of saying yes ("Ya, mon")

"Porfa" - Abbreviation of "Por Favor", meaning "Please"

2. Eat Like a Local - Breakfast

Guatemalan cuisine is one of the best in Central America; their breakfast in particular is one of their delicacies. This meal is referred to as "Desayuno Tipico" or "Desayuno Chapin".

A tipico (typical) breakfast usually includes:

- Black beans

- Fried plantains

- Eggs, usually scrambled or fried

- Fresh cheese

- Tortillas

- Chirmol (a type of tomato sauce)

- Occasionally meat in the form of sausages or steak
slices

You can easily make this yourself, due to its simple - but tasty - nature, sourcing the ingredients fresh from the local market (see Tip 16). However, don't worry if you're not a natural in the kitchen, you can find this breakfast in any of the hundreds of cafes that are dotted along the streets. The best and most authentic I have found is in *Santa Clara,* a sweet little bakery and rooftop cafe on 2nd Avenida Sur, serving traditional breakfast, with Guatemalan coffee, all day long.

3. Eat like a Local - Lunch and Dinner

As you will notice during your time in Antigua, traditional food is made mostly from the same ingredients, reworked in different styles for each meal. Mostly, dishes will contain a form of black beans, avocado, carne (meat) and tortillas.

However, there is one typical lunch time dish that steps away from this trend; Pepian.

Pepian has now become known as the national dish of Guatemala. It is a filling and hearty stew, made with meat, local vegetables, seeds and potatoes. You will find it on every traditional menu and even sold on the streets served from giant cooking pots into paper bowls.

Guatemalans like their food spiced, don't worry though, the food is rarely ever spicy - in Latin America its all about the flavour. If you prefer your food slightly milder, just ask, the people are friendly and are always happy to help.

Also on the streets you will find guatemalan versions of quesidilas, toastadas, tacos, and tortillas de harina (similar to burritos). Again, these are usually filled with the staples: beans, avocado, onion, tomato and meat. Usually prepared fresh right in front of you!

In my opinion, the best thing about street food is that they are available at any time of day and night. First thing in the morning keep your eyes peeled for Chile Rellenos and Tortillas being sold outside of the Tiendas, and later in the day head to the main square for some guacamole covered Toastadas or tasty Shucos. During the evening, perhaps after a few drinks at one of the local bars, pick up some street tacos from the friendly vendors for a delicious late night snack!

4. Eat like a Local - Desserts

Guatemalan desserts are arguably some of the best in Central America. Whilst other countries specialize in alcohol and sugar covered cakes, the Guatemalans are proved themselves far more inventive when it comes to sweet treats.

Rellenitos de Platano

Possibly the most intriguing of the dessert options, Rellenitos are made of only plantains, sugar and black beans. The plantains are cooked, pureed and hand crafted into a handy little oval shape. They are then filled with black beans that have been cooked down to a paste and then sweetened. The whole thing is then rolled in sugar and cinnamon, proving that beans and plantains are the perfect combination for both the savory and sweet toothed traveler.

Mole

Another plantain-based dessert, mole is traditional consumed at Christmas but can be found all year round. Mole is essentially fried plantains in a chili-chocolate sauce, usually sprinkled with pumpkin and/or sesame seeds. This is a rich and filling dessert so make sure you leave some room post-tacos!

5. Cook Like a Local

Once you've tried all Guatemala's delicious and original meals, you may be intrigued about how to prepare them yourself. Antigua is home to many high quality cooking schools that will teach you how to prepare, cook and serve traditional food like a local Guatemalteco! Some Spanish schools also offer free cooking classes in the afternoons (see Tip 6).

El Frijol Feliz

Since its opening in 2007, El Frijol Feliz (or in English - The Happy Bean) has been teaching students traditional Guatemalan culinary skills to take home. The classes are small in number and taught by working chefs - experts in Guatemalan cuisine. Not only does EFF offer classes but it also takes its students on culinary tours to encourage learning about the origin and nature of each ingredient.

La Tortilla

La Tortilla states that there is no better way to learn about a culture than through its cuisine - and they are not wrong! They offers classes, courses and tours, acknowledging your food journey by gifting you with an official certificate at the end! With classes running twice daily in the morning and the afternoon, it will be easy to find a time to suit your schedule.

6. Go to Spanish School

Antigua is somewhat famous on the traveler trail for its collection of Spanish Schools both inside and surrounding the city.

For an small fee you can study Spanish from 3-6 hours a day, and for a little more you can stay with a friendly Guatemala family who will prepare you three delicious meals a day from Monday-Saturday, and help you on your Spanish speaking journey.

Immersion is without a doubt the best way to learn a new langauge. The teachers are all Guatemalan, dedicated to getting you speaking as quickly and as efficently as possible. Immersing yourself like this is a great way to learn and experience the language, the food and the culture.

What's more, if you're planning on traveling through Latin America or even just staying in Antigua for a while, then this is a great way to learn some useful phrases from local people (see Tip 1)!

7. Learn how to Salsa

No matter how long you spend in Antigua, you will quickly learn that dancing is huge part of the culture. There are classes and dances on almost every night of the week and people take their time on the dance floor very seriously.

Whether you have two left feet or you are already gifted in the art of salsa dancing - Antigua has something to offer you. There are two main dancing schools and both offer free classes once a week - so there is no excuse not to bring your dancing shoes.

Even if you have never danced before, you will be encouraged again and again to get out of your comfort zone, let go of your inhibitions and twirl around the dance floor until the early hours of the morning.

Many of the Spanish Schools also offer weekly afternoon lessons for free, providing you with an excellent chance to practice some of your new found linguistic skills, to make new friends and to experience Antigua in a social environment.

8. Find Where to Dance Salsa

There is always salsa dancing happening somewhere in Antigua, and you don't have to look very hard to find it. Follow the sounds of the Latin American music and soon you will come across a jam-packed dance floor full of sweaty bodies spinning and moving to the rhythms. As you enter you will notice that the space is filled with locals, expats and tourists alike, proving that cultural dances can bring people together from all walks of life.

La Sin Ventura

Every Tuesday night in the hotel and restaurant La Sin Ventura, there is a salsa dancing bonanza. They provide a live band and a dance floor, with both experienced and non-experienced dancers taking advantage of the space and the music. The band plays a mixture of salsa, bachata, merengue and cumbia until about 11:30pm when they are replaced by a

DJ playing commercial Latin American music. La Sin Ventura is a great place for dancer, non-dancers, locals and tourists. It is a social hub and melting pot of culture and activity where anything can happen!

La Sala

La Sala Bar is one of the most poplar dance clubs in Antigua. Every Sunday night it holds a salsa night, with optional lessons before the more serious dancing starts. Similar to La Sin Ventura, the night starts with a live band, before moving on to reggaeton music played by local DJs.

9. Navigate the Cobblestone Streets

The layout of Antigua can be daunting for a new arrival. Luckily the town itself is fairly small and almost everything is in walking distance of each other. The logic of the layout is a tricky one to get your head around, but once you have, navigation is a breeze. The town is made up of streets (calles) and avenues (avenidas) and are labelled as either east (oriente), west (poniente), north (norte) or south (sur), in relation to Central Park.

Confused? Thankfully, the roads are clearly marked and go in number order. Go for walks, get lost a couple of times, it is almost impossible to leave Antigua without realising it. You will soon be comfortable with navigating the cobblestone jungle.

10. Learn how to Farm

If you have some free time and want to give something back to the community, head down to Coaba Farm. Located at the end of 5th. Avienda Sur (5th Avenue South), the farm is a little slice of permaculture heaven.

They also have an organic cafe which serves food grown on site, live music and a farmers market every weekend. Go to connect with like-minded individuals and the support the local community. Everyone that attends always has something interesting to say, and are always eager to listen and learn.

What's more, Caoba welcome traveling volunteers with open arms! You don't need any prior experience, they will teach you how to farm, build, weed and grow. Its a perfect way to spend some time in nature, practice your Spanish, and learn a new skill. For just two hours work, they give you a gigantic bag of fresh vegetables to take home for your own table!

11. Explore Rooftop Hangouts

Undoubtedly the best way to admire the magnificent skyline of Antigua is from up high. You can watch the hustle and bustle of the streets and admire the backdrop of the beautiful volcanoes at sunset whilst enjoying a drink and maybe even a loaded plate of nachos.

Cafe Sky

Cafe Sky is a beautiful spot to head to either in the evenings or the mornings when it is slightly cooler. This is probably the highest rooftop in the city and gives you an unrivaled panoramic view of the volcanoes and the streets.

Frank & Fre

A hostel/bar with a relaxing rooftop space filled with comfortable chairs and sofas is a great place to head if you need a rest after exploring the city. They serve both typical and exotic food, as well as alcoholic beverages, such as beer, wine and cocktails.

Luna De Miel

Possibly one of the most delicious spots in Antigua. Luna de Miel serves sweet and savory crepes, of all different shapes and sizes and with many different fillings (try the warm spinach, honey, pine nut and goats cheese). You can enjoy your pancakes out on the beautiful rooftop terrance, but usually only if you are prepared to queue!

12. Find out about Guatemalan History

Antigua is rich with culture. Take advantage of the many museums (see Tip 11) and heritage sites around to learn about the history of the city and of the country itself.

By talking to locals and exploring the ruins you can learn about everything from the Spanish conquest to the earthquakes and volcanoes that changed the very landscape of the city.

Antigua Guatemala, literally translates as Ancient Guatemala, and once stood proud as the third capital of the country. Overtime, the city has been destroyed by volcano eruptions and earthquakes, until eventually the status of capital was moved to Guatemala City, where it still stands now.

13. Go to the Art Exhibitions and Museums

Explore and enjoy the many museums and art galleries that Antigua has to often. The city has everything ranging from chocolate museums to jade museums.

La Antigua Art Gallery houses beautiful and unique collections by artists from Guatemala, Central America and the Caribbean. It features both paintings and sculptures and it a hotspot for contemporary art in Guatemala.

The Museo de Arte Colonial (Museum of Colonial Art), established in 1936, has a large collection of art ranging from the 16th-18th centuries. There are some 133 works inside, all saturated with historical and cultural essence. Visiting transporting you back in time to colonial Guatemala, and opens your imagination to the experience of Antigua hundreds of years ago.

14. Watch Interesting Documentaries whilst Eating Bagels

The Bagel Barn, located just a few meters away from Central Park, not only sells delicious bagels, smoothies and juices (including Kombucha!), but it also shows free movies everyday!

The Bagel Barn shows films and documentaries in both English and Spanish with opposing subtitles, usually about cultural and eye-opening topics. Get there on time to get a good seat and order your bagel in time for the film to start.

15. Learn what 'Los Tres Tiempos' Actually Means

On every street above the Tienda - a little like a corner shop - you will see a sign stating "Los Tres Tiempos". In spanish this literally translates to 'The Three Times', which doesn't really make sense. What this actually means, is that this Tienda sells freshly made tortillas three times a day, at breakfast, lunch and dinner.

If you pass by at these times you will see one or two women in traditional Mayan dress hand making little soft tortillas. There usually sell at around 1 Quetzal for 5 fresh tortillas. They are a delicious accompaniment to any meal, and a staple of the Guatemalan diet.

16. Explore the Market - Food

The main market is difficult to miss. It is situated on 4th Calle Poniente (4th Street West) and has everything from electricals to clothes to food.

The food section is by far the biggest. You can enjoy a multitude of exotic fresh fruit and vegetables, fish, meat and staples such as lentils, rice and beans. Shopping here is much cheaper than shopping at the super markets or Tiendas, and not to mention a much more exciting and colorful experience.

It can be a little overwhelming at first due to the noise of the hagglers and the sellers, and the sheer amount of people. However, once you have been a few times, each visit becomes a new adventure. You will learn how to haggle for a cheaper prices, how to identify all the different kinds of mangoes and the spanish names for all the different spices.

Spending an hour in the market is surely one of the greatest learning experiences in the city.

17. Explore the Market - Artisan

There are two main artisan markets in the city. One is located right next to the main market, and the other is behind the famous *Pollo Campero*, near Central Park. The latter is a tourist destination, which is far cleaner and easier to navigate than the main market, but is also slightly more expensive.

In the artisan markets you will find masses upon masses of colourful mayan items. There are backpacks, shoes, jewelry, bags, clothing, everything you can imagine, with a mayan twist. You can haggle here too, prices are competitive but don't settle for the first price they give you. Haggle correctly and you will come away with beautiful cost effective gifts for your friends and family back home, and maybe even something for yourself.

18. Climb Volcano Pacaya

Surrounding Antigua are three majestic volcanoes, Pacaya, Acatenango and Agua. Pacaya is the smallest of the three, the hike to the top takes about one and a half hours and once you get to there you can unwind by roasting marshmallows over hot lava.

If you're not feeling brave enough to do the overnight hike to the top of Acatenango, but still want the thrills of climbing an active volcano, then Pacaya is your best bet. At the top, stunning views and nature will accompany the feeling of great achievement. Don't forget to pack hiking boots!

19. Climb Volcano Acatenango

Climbing Volcan Acatenango is definitely a challenge, but if you are up for it, it is more than worth it. It is an overnight trek, with 7 hours climb up the mountain and 4 hours back down again the next day. At the top of the Volcano you will wake up to watch the sunrise over Volcan Aqua, and if you're lucky, will see some lava erupting from its summit.

Most companies you book through will supply you with a tent, a sleeping bag and food. However, you will need to provide water, snacks and warm clothes (trust me you will need them). Like most things that take a lot of hard work, the reward is great. In fact, if you have the stamina, this experience is one of the most rewarding that you will encounter in Antigua.

20. Where to Stay

Antigua has somewhere to stay for every budget. There are budget hostels that go as cheap as 30Q per night, and mid-range to costly, yet beautiful, hotels. There are also a number of guest houses and families who will give you a comfortable room, and potentially cooked meals, for a weekly rate.

Porta Hotel Antigua, is an eco-conscious, five star hotel dedicated to sustainability and promoting eco-friendly tourism. They have fitness facilities, excursions, a pool and they allow you to bring a maximum of one pet! Rooms are around $140/night

On the other end of the scale, you have hostels like The Three Monkeys. Run by backpackers, this hostel is not short of colour or character. It has a small rooftop with a couple of sofas to enuoy the afternoon sunshine, a T.V room, laundry service and a kitchen. A shared dorm with an en-suite starts at around $9/night.

There are so many different options when it comes to accommodation in Antigua, whatever your budget may be - you will be spoilt for choice.

21. Keeping Fit

Keeping fit - every travelers nemesis. How do you enjoy all those refried beans, tacos and freshly picked avocados without putting on a few pounds? Luckily Antigua has a few options.

There are a few gyms in Antigua and some of the hotels have their own fitness facilities, but the best external gym by far is *Antigua's Gym.* There is a gym floor, a selection of

machines and a weekly timetable of different classes,

including TRX and Zumba! They have price options to suit

every traveler and resident, but usually for one week

membership is $15, and for a month it is $34. The way it is

run is very modern, the trainers are friendly and the space is

kept clean and well-maintained.

If thats not enough you can always go for a run up to the

Cerro de la Cruz (more on this in tip 31), or take a few

sweaty salsa lessons (see tip 7)!

22. Where to Find the Best Coffee

Guatemala is famous for its coffee. It exports

worldwide, supplying most notably to the high-street giants -

Starbucks! It is clear when you're there that you are spoilt for choice. In fact, you could probably have a cup of coffee from a different place for two wholes weeks and not be disappointed once.

A few of my favorites are:

- The Refuge Coffee Bar

- Cafe Boheme

- GuateJava Roastery and Coffeehouse

- Fernandos Kaffee.

23. Getting Out of Antigua

Although Antigua is beautiful is many ways, it is very easy to get stuck here and not explore the other wonders that Guatemala has to offer, and it is certainly not short of them!

Locals get around the country on Chicken Buses, although in my opinion these are only for the experienced traveler. If you are not yet comfortable on these up-cycled American school buses, then you can easily book a shuttle to almost any other tourist destination in Guatemala from Antigua.

There are booking offices on pretty much every street, and all quote relatively similar prices, usually in USD.

The best places to get a shuttle to are:

- Semuc Champey *nature preserve*

- Lake Atitlan

- Izabal *Lake, Puerto Barrios, Livingston*

- Monterico *black sand beach, Pacific*
  (Turtles Aug- Nov only) so so

24. Where to Shop

In the market you will find good quality, cheap second hand clothes and shoes, not forgetting all the artisan handcrafts which make wonderful gifts from friends and family. However, if you are looking for something more upmarket yet still with that authentic touch, then head over to the streets surrounding Central Park; my personal favorite for shopping is 4th Avenida sur.

Adorning these streets you will find high quality independent boutiques, jewelers, art supplies and much more. This is a good place to pick up some jade jewelry, at Casa del Jade, some guatemalan folk inspired fine art at aptly named, Casa de Artes, or some beautiful handcrafted clothes and accessories at Uxibal. Expect to pay western prices at all these stores, although it is well worth the price tag!

Also lining these streets you will find many cafes serving a wide range of delicious foods, perfect for a spot of lunch while you shop. Fear not vegans and vegetarians, there is plenty of choice for you too! Check out Samsara - a completely vegan (and delicious) cafe. I recommend the tofu tacos, accompanied with a sweet potato and cacao smoothie. More on where to eat in tip 28.

25. Drink at the Best Bars

As a tourist and traveler hotspot, Antigua is certainly not short of watering holes. There is the almost famous Cafe No Se, which serves high quality Mescal, be careful though, those of you who have tried it know that this is a dangerous drink. Cafe No Se has a smoky, mystical atmosphere, the space is narrow and separated by small doors, giving it an almost Alice-in-wonderland feel. The bar is always lined with interesting people passing through the city, expect to meet people from all over the world and in exciting professions. It is open until late so it is a popular spot at any time of the night, and the clientele certainly varies depending on what hour of the night you enter.

Just down the road you will find lesser known but equally as fascinating, *Por Que No?* It is hidden on the corner of 2 Avenida Sur and 9 Calle Oriente, with no clear signage. However you will be able to recognize it by the lights and chatter coming from inside. The food and the drinks - which is mostly just beer and wine - are simple and delicious, and the staff are friendly and welcoming. You will struggle to find another place like it in the busy city.

Also worth a mention are for their drinks menu are Cafe Sky and Las Vibras, expect to find all the usual suspects and some more unusual ones too.

26. Where to Eat

Now you have the low down on whats good to eat on the street, you're probably wondering where to find something that hasn't been cooked roadside. Just like accommodation, there is nutrition for every budget.

On the cheaper side of things, there is small cafe/restaurant *Y Tu Piña, Tambien.* They serve tasty smoothies, filling sandwiches, and american, british and guatemalan breakfasts! It is quiet, cosy and casual, and like *Cafe No Se*, usually seats interesting and well-traveled people.

Mid-range cost-wise, you will find El Viejo Cafe. With its beautiful patio eating area, shrouded in exotic green plants, it feels like you are eating in a little slice of paradise. It is run by locals, serving both traditional Guatemalan food and more american items, like hamburgers and sandwiches. I recommend a traditional breakfast of fried eggs, chorizo, beans, plantains, fresh cheese, bread and Guatemalan coffee - all for 49Q (about $7)!

For a more upmarket experience, head to *Los Tres Tiempos*. It not only has a unique mayan-inspired inside eating area, but it also has a delectable terrace. Whats great about Los Tre Tiempos, is that it is committed to sharing Guatemalan culture. They prepare dishes that are typical of various different locations in Guatemala, including Livingston - a town on the Caribbean side, where to locals dine on coconut breaded shrimp and Caribbean salsa.

Because Antigua is city where many different cultures meet, collide and influence, it is also a city rich in culinary culture. A little exploring and you will find indian cuisine, sushi, local food, american food and Chinese food - all prepared and created to a high, authentic standard.

27. Take a Walk Through Parque Central

Surrounded by majestic colonial architecture, and abundant in travelers and locals alike throughout the year, Central Park - or Parque Central - perfectly encapsulates the meaning of the heart of the city. In the center giant stone mermaids stand in the middle of a fountain - a remodel of the original created in the early 1700's.

Women in traditional Mayan dress walk together whilst their children play, teasing the pigeons that flock in the square. Taking a walk through this special park takes you fluidly through centuries and centuries of history. From the buildings surrounding the park, to the sheer diversity of people that wander through there, Parque Central makes us feels like time and location are illusions of the modern world.

28. Discover the Churches

Despite being a relatively small city, Antigua is home to around 35 practicing churches. The most magnificent of these is Iglesia de la Mercad, bright yellow in colour and decorated with intricate adornments on its white columns, it catches the eye of a passerby instantaneously.

As well as the churches, there are also a number of convents that are worth exploring, most notably the Santo Domingo Convent. Previously the biggest and richest monastery in the country, it is now part of the *Casa Santo Domingo Hotel.* The original structure was founded in 1542 and there are still some of the original building inside the hotel.

29. Hike up to Cerro de la Cruz

Cerro de la Cruz is the perfect viewpoint looking down over the city and the volcanoes. It is a bit of a hike up, you climb what feels like a thousand steps to get to the top, but it is worth the walk.

Once you get to the top you can quench your thirst a spicy granizado, an drink of frozen shaved ice and a selection of fruits and spices, usually flavored with lemon and pepita. This concoction may seem bizarre to the usual Westerner, but to Guatemalatecos, this beverage is a usual treat, especially for children. From the top of the Cerro you can see out over the whole of the city and the towns surrounding it. In the evening, if you time it right you can bask in the evening sunlight and you watch the spectacle of the sun disappearing behind the volcanoes.

30. Discover The Ruins

Taking the time to explore some of the ruins, quite literally feels like you have gone back in time. All built between the 16th-18th century, there are 6 main attractions in the city and you can easily spend an entire day learning and exploring them.

Most are old churches and monasteries that were destroyed by the many terrible earthquakes that shook the city in the early 18th century. Of course, because of its geography, earthquakes are still frequent in Antigua, although none as destructive as the quakes of it's past.

The Main ruins are:

- The Ruins of Recollection

- San Jeronimo Ruins

- Capuchins Monestary

- Church of Santa Domingo

- Ruins of Santa Rosa

- Ruins of The Church of Candelaria

All the ruins conveniently stand along a 90 degree route, starting at the end of 1st Calle Poniente, continuing along the entire road and then turning right on to 1 Avenida Norta, which ultimately take you up to the Cerro (tip 30). During your stay in Antigua, spend a day exploring the ruins, then ending at the Cerro for a breathtaking sunset.

31. Learn About The Mayans

Guatemala itself has the highest population of indigenous people out of all the countries in Central America, with traditional Maya people making up half of the overall population count. As you travel through the country, you will notice that they are not limited to the more rural areas. In the capital city and Antigua alike, you can see many Mayans in traditional dress, still taking part in traditional Mayan activities, and conversing in one of the many ancient Mayan languages.

Antigua provides you with the rare opportunity to explore and learn about an ancient culture from the comfort of a busy city. Many of the indigenous people of Guatemala suffer discrimination, particularly in the workplace. With the majority of Mayan adults being illiterate, and most of their children never attending school, it is becoming increasingly difficult for them to find work in an society moving away from a traditional way a life.

If the Mayans and their way of life interest you, or you feel as though you can offer you services to indigenous communities, Antigua has many options for both voluntary and paid work - depending on your skills and previous experience.

Many American students live in Antigua and commute to Guatemala City to volunteer working with indigenous children. If the commute does not appeal to you there are also many organisations in and surrounding Antigua, who are always looking for volunteers.

Volunteering is a great way to experience Antigua through a different lens. It allows you insights into life in the city through working with and forming relationships with local people. Ultimately, there is no better way to experience a culture than through working with its people.

32. Buy Beautiful Jade

Jade (pronounced in Spanish as "ha-day") is a beautiful rock, found throughout Guatemala and its surrounding countries. The ancient Mayans, one of the first known civilizations to use Jade, valued it immensely and out of it they crafted tools, ornaments and artifacts. Jade is formed out of many interlocking crystals and has been used throughout history, by the Mayans, ancient Chinese cultures and the Romans, to cure kidney disease.

Guatemalan Jade - also known as "Jadeite" - is the rarest

form of Jade and comes in a selection of greens, ranging from bright and luminous, to dark and stormy. It was described by the Mayans as a gift from Heaven - "la piedra del cielo".

In Antigua there are jade shops on almost every road, including inside the Artisan Market. You can purchase everything from jewelry to ornaments, and even replicas of Mayan gods and goddesses. There is also the Jade Museum - Casa Del Jade - which presents both jade in its natural states, and in forms that reflects the magnificent craftsmanship of the ancient Mayans. The museum takes you on a journey through time, informing you not only of jade and its mystical qualities, but also about the lives and mysteries of the Mayans.

33. Eat Guatemalan Chocolate

If you love chocolate, then Antigua is the right place for you. There are many delightful little sweet and chocolate shops dotted around the city. Inside you will find fruits dipped in chocolate, decadent filled truffles and much more. Then to top it all off on 4a Calle Oreinte there is the Choco Museo (The Chocolate Museum), which celebrates everything central-american cacao. There are products both edible and non edible, including chocolate covered coffee beans, face masks and body scrubs.

As you enter the shop you will be instantly intoxicated by the smell of rich, organic chocolate seeping through the packaging. Guatemalans take great pride in their chocolate, and most of the cacao they use in the shop is bought from the pacific coast of the country, whilst everything in the museum is made, by hand, on the premises.

Cacao has become somewhat of a buzzword in mainstream Western culture recently, with a rising interest in healthy, natural and organic foods. The word cacao originally comes from the Mayan word 'ka'kau', which they believed was discovered by the Gods. The Mayan kings ate cacao, calling it 'the food of love', and even now, the chocolate eaten by many guatemalans is prepared in the same way - by being fermented first.

34. Experience The Views at El Tenedor

Part of the Casa Santo Domingo - El Tenedor is a beautiful restaurant situated high up one of the mountains surrounding Antigua.

There is a free shuttle once every hour from the Hotel Santo Domingo, which takes you up to the grounds in which

El Tenedor is situated. Once you arrive, you can wander through the grounds that are filled with beautiful nature, art - both inside and outside, museums, a grand church, a zip line and artisan crafts for sale. All the art and museums are paying homage to contemporary Guatemalan artists and writer, who tackle current issues that are prevalent not only in Guatemala, but also throughout Central America.

Once you get to the restaurant you can sit either inside or outside, and enjoy the views of Antigua below and the Volcán de Agua from across the city. They serve Italian, American and Guatemalan food, sourcing most of the ingredients and herbs from the surrounding gardens. Although it is on the more expensive side, it is definitely an unmissable feature of the city, hidden high up on the mountain side.

35. Where to go Out-Out

Antigua may seem like a traditional colonial city, inhabited by Mayans and rich with culture, but do not be fooled. The modern day Guatemalans, travelers and expats all know how to through a party, and when they come together, you get a vibrant mix of culture and music that will please everyone.

Monoloco

Monoloco is a restaurant and bar that turns into club after hours. It ismostly classed as an ex-pat sports bar, which truthfully, it is. The perfect hangout for travelers, where the staff all speak english and the food is classic western with a central american twist - try their loaded nachos, they are delicious. Despite it not being authentic central american style, many Guatemalans still go and enjoy the days and nights here.

Las Vibras

Open every evening from wednesday through to saturday, Las Vibras in the biggest, and busiest, night club in Antigua. It has weekly ladies nights and themed parties, playing a mix of latin-american music, and western dance music. Be prepared, dancing is a big part of Guatemalan culture and they are not at all shy on the dance floor of Las Vibras.

36. Places for Writing

If you are a traveling nomad, a student, or simply like to keep up to date with your emails whilst you are abroad, a decent WiFi spot with good coffee is probably of high importance to you. Antigua, being the forward thinking city that it is, has literally hundreds of good place for relaxing with some free WiFi and beverage. Whilst pretty much everywhere offers a decent wifi connection these days, its just as important to pick somewhere that makes focusing on your work just that little bit easier.

My favorite place to get down and dirty with my workload was Union Cafe, located on 6a Calle Oriente, right by Parque Unión. Great for the health conscious traveler as inside you will find delicious and healthy smoothies, acaí bowls, vegan treats and guatemalan coffee with a selection of both dairy and non-dairy milks. The walls are decorated with contemporary central america artworks, that are also all for sale. However, the best thing about this place is that the Wifi also connects across the street in the Park. So you can buy your smoothie, set a blanket down in the park, open your laptop and get to work.

Another great place to get connected is at Rainbow Cafe. Famous for its affordable yet delicious food (with lots of vegetarian and gluten free options!), it also has a small bookshop attached, selling literature in a variety of different languages. In the evenings there are also talks and lectures about getting involved in humanitarian and environmental projects current at work in Guatemala. This highly educational and open-minded place provides the perfect atmosphere to concentrate at your online tasks.

37. Take A Photo Under The Arc

During a quick google search of the city, or a flick through the 'Antigua' section of a travel book, you will undoubtably see a picture of a majestic colonial yellow arc. Its location is on the busiest, most touristic street of Antigua - 5th Avenida Norte, becoming somewhat of a landmark, and the most photographed street in the city. The arc is actually called *Santa Catalina Arch,* built in the 17th century in order to connect the Santa Catalina covent to its neighboring school, providing the nuns with a safe passage over the busy streets.

Adorning the sides of the road on 5th Avenida Norte there are street artists and Mayan women selling traditional Mayan clothing and gifts. Along this street you will also notice many shops selling usual Guatemalan goods, such as, Jade, Coffee and Chocolate. The only downside is that the street is very busy during the day, but heading down for sunrise is the ideal time to get a picture. The Santa Catalina Arch, and the side of the old covent is bathed in beautiful morning light, and the normally hectic street is almost silent apart from a the birds waking up for the day. In the silence and serenity of the morning, you can get a glorious photo of Antigua's most iconic building.

38. Join In the Parades

Throughout the year there are festivals, celebrations and parades that take place in Antigua. During these times the city comes alive with bright colors, food and festivities. As most Guatemalans are devote christians, these festivals have their roots in religion but are executed with a vibrant latin american flare.

Semana Santa (Easter Holy Week)

Semana Santa takes place during the week leading up to Easter, and like all other christian countries, is concerned with the death and resurrection of Jesus Christ. It is unquestionably the most exciting and elaborate festival that takes place in Antigua. During this time the residents in Guatemala hang beautifully decorated curtains and cloths as well as paper decorations on the front of their houses, to symbolise the suffering and resurrection of Jesus. On palm sunder there is also a large procession through the street, with giant floats telling the story of Easter, including live music, delicious food, drinks and street games.

Burning of the Devil

On the 7th of december every year, large crowds gather

in Antigua to burn the devil. Paper maché devils are available for purchase in the local market, for those who wish to personally participate in the event. Residents dress up in devil horns and clothing, in a night that is similar to halloween, as they swarm round a giant wooden statue of the devil himself. This tradition started in colonial times, when the rich would place lanterns outside their homes before the celebration of the Virgin Mary. The poor, who could not afford the lanterns, instead burnt rubbish outside the front of their homes. This practice eventually evolved into what is now known as the burning of the devil.

39. Drink Local Hot Chocolate

As previously mentioned in tip 34, Guatemalans are extremely proud of their cacao and chocolate. However, most Guatemalans don't eat chocolate, instead, they drink it. It is a particularly popular drink during christmas, when drinking chocolate and eating tamales is a traditional christmas meal.

Lots of cafes sell the tradtional chocolate drink, and for just 10Q, you can buy slabs of chocolate that can be melted into hot water and enjoyed - much better than the powder variation we are used to in the wester world.

The best way to make this delicious drink at home, is to buy around 2 tablets of the guatemalan pressed cacao (also great to nibble at on its own but try to resist!), and boil it in a pan of water with one cinnamon stick and a pinch of salt. The traditional way to enjoy this is without milk, however, if you can imagine your hot chocolate without it, you can substitute the water for milk. Bring the ingredients to a slow boil in the pan, stirring continuously and serve immediately once the chocolate is completely dissolved.

40. When To Visit

The climate in Guatemala its fairly consistent all year round, and it is often referred to as The Land of Eternal Spring because of its comfortable conditions. Obviously conditions vary slightly throughout the year and location. However in Antigua, the climate is generally pleasant all year.

There is a rainy season that lasts from May-October, but it is sunny apart from an hour of two in the afternoon when there will be some rainfall. The dry season lasts from November - May, where there is virtually no rainfall and the temperature is in the low twenties most days; perfect for outdoor ventures. Be warned though, in Antigua during the winter months (December-January), temperatures can drop very low in the evening, sometimes below 5 degrees Celsius! If you are here during theses months, it is advisable to pack some warm clothes. If you arrive with none, there are heaps of second hand jumpers and coats in the market (see tips)

The rest of Guatemala does not differ too much in climate. Petén - the location of the Ancient city of *Tikal* - sees the most rainfall during the rainy season. Whilst the coastal regions are generally warmer that the rest of the country, with temperatures sometimes reaching as high as 37 degrees! In these areas there is also little change in temperature between day and night.

Guatemala is beautiful and comfortable to travel all year round. The busiest time to go is between December - May, when there is less rain and lower temperatures. Traveling outside these times means less crowds but also more unpredictable rainfall.

41. What Currency to Take

The Quetzal is the national currency used in Guatemala, and probably the most unique and interesting out of all the countries in central america because of its rich history.

As well as being a form of money, a quetzal is the national bird of Guatemala. It is vibrant colours of green, gold and red, with long green tails that are almost double the length of their bodies. The bird proudly serves as the symbol in the center of the Guatemalan flag.

In Mayan times the bird was a considered extremely sacred. Its feathers were used as decoration, clothing and currency. However, hunting of the bird for feathers was forbidden, and the Mayans and Aztecs only traded with feathers they found on the forest floor.

Unfortunately, due to deforestation happening across the country, the number of Quetzals are in steady decline.

Humans have started hunting them for feathers, despite this being banned by the ancient civilizations to which the land belonged.

The best place to look for the remaining Quetzals is in the forests of Petén, in the thick woodland that they share with toucans, monkeys and jaguars.

42. Relax with some Yoga and Meditation

Even in a small city like Antigua, city life can take its toll. Sometimes you need to check out of your routine and check in with yourself. Lake Atitlan, a few hours away from Antigua, is filled with yoga ashrams, retreats and meditation centers, and its ethos has spread over to the cobblestones of Antigua.

Nomad Yoga Shala

Situated about five minutes out of town but inexpensive to reach in a tuk-tuk, Nomand Yoga Shala offers traditional Ashtanga Mysore. Class takes place in a beautiful natural lit studio with large windows. Mats, blocks and even showers are provided. This place is perfect for a yogi with experience who is looking for a regular spot to practice.

YogAntigua

YogAntigua is great because of its teachers. Their teachers, who come from all over the world, all have long histories of yoga practice in many different styles, the classes are taught in a mix of spanish and english and are taking by travelers, expats and locals alike. They offer morning and afternoon prices in two beautiful locations in the city - one an art gallery, and the other a hotel rooftop. What's more, they have classes for beginners and intimidate practitioners, gentle yoga and power yoga, yoga for the elderly and pre-natal yoga. When it comes to YogAntigua, there really is something to please everyone.

43. Dine Outside

The climate in Antigua, especially during the dry season, if perfect for dining outside at any time during the day. Three of my favourite spots, although all slightly off the beaten track, are abundant with breathtaking nature, delicious food and stunning views.

Caoba Cafe

As mentioned in Tip 10, Caoba Farm is a self sustaining eco-farm, employing local people and paying volunteers with giant bags of fresh vegetables.

Near the front entrance of the farm, surrounded by exotic plants and flowers, sits the Caoba Cafe. Everything on the menu is grown and prepared on site, and they have a selection of vegan, vegetarian and meat based dishes. Pizza is their speciality, although they also serve breakfast, burgers, sandwiches and salads.

Earthlodge

An delectable eco-friendly farm, hotel and restaurant situated high up on the mountain side and focused on growing avocados. Providing views of the volcanoes, hand-built tree houses and home-cooked food. You can get to the restaurant via a pleasant downhill walk, but be prepared that the walk back up can be quite tedious.

Hobbitenango

Yet another mountain side hotel and restaurant, Hobbitenango is unique as it is based on the Hobbit town - The Shire - from the famous Lord of The Rings novels. If you chose to stay here, you can stay in little home with circle doors built directly into the mountain-side. Even the menu is inspired by the Tolkien books, serving both first breakfast and second breakfast. Dining here means outside seating on the edge of the mountain looking out at the green valleys below, dreaming of dragons, wizards and far away lands.

44. Drink Like a Local

As far as beers go, there is only one in Guatemala that you should be drinking, Gallo. The national beer of the country, brewed in the capital city and named after a rooster, any guatemalan will tell you that this is the best beer in central america. It is sold in every bar and Tienda in Antigua, you don't have to look far or hard to find it.

For something a little stronger and just as local, Quetzalteca is your best bet, and its hard to miss. Sold in a range of sizes, it is distinct by its glass bottle with an indigenous woman in the front, known locally as La Indita. Made from raw cane sugar, it comes in three flavours, original - of which the taste is hard to describe, tamarindo, and rosa de jamaica (also known as hibiscus). Quetzalteca is a dangerous liquor, not for the faint heartend, locals tend to by the medium size bottle and down two or three right there and then in the store.

Alcoholism is serious issue in Guatemala, especially among the indigenous communities. During your time in Antigua you will most likely see a few locals face down in doorways and on street corners. The locals call them boros, or borrachos, which essentially means drunk. The boros are more often than not, completely harmless. My advice is not to try and keep us with the locals, but to explore the bars and different drinks are your own pace

45. Find a Taste of Home

Living, traveling or even just holidaying abroad can sometimes make you feel homesick. Antigua has a lot to offer for when that wave of longing for home seems to seep into your psyche. One of the best ways to connect with a place far away is through your stomach. When you taste a certain cuisine you are transported to its country of origin, finding comfort through your senses.

In Antigua not only will you find the usual suspects; Mcdonalds, Wendys, Starbucks, Subway - and many more in the global fast food industy, but you will also find options that are a little more gourmet, or a little more authentic.

Ganesh Restaurant

Authentic and delicious Indian cuisine, of course, Indian food doesn't just remind us of India. Those of you traveling from the UK will be more than comfortable identifying most of the items on the menu, and you won't be disappointed in the taste either. Ganesh provides international favourites, including; samosas, popular curries and naan bread.

Reilly's

It seems impossible to find a popular holiday destination that does not have an Irish Sports Bar. Reilly's serves drinks, bar food, and shows big sporting events. The bar staff and owners and friendly, and inside you will find travelers and expats from all over the world, coming together over a few pints of comforting home brew.

The Londoner

Another little pub nestled into the side of 6th Avenida Norte. The Londoner is an authentic, british owned joint, great to get a seat in if you are craving a decent pub lunch.

46. Get Out of Antigua - Lake Atitlan

A few hours away from Antigua via shutte bus and stamped firmly into the traveler trail and the expat map, Lake Atitlan is home to Mayans, Guatemalans, expats and tourists alike. Internationally known for its outstanding natural beauty, Atitlan is a must-see destination when visiting Guatemala.

Lake Atitlan, is a large, picturesque lake, surrounded by volcanoes, small villages and backpacker towns - complete with hikes, nature trails, wildlife, bars and yoga ashrams - it really is a strange yet magical place. There are three main towns that travelers and expats usually congregate towards ; San Pedro, San Marcos and Panajachel. Each one has its own feel and specific clientele, and each is just as beautiful and captivating as the next. Take some time to explore all the Lake and the people there have to offer and you won't be disappointed.

47. Get Out of Antigua - Chichicastenango

Chichicastenango Market, held on Thursdays and Sundays, can only be described as a melting pot of beautiful, somewhat-organised, chaos.

A short ride away from Antigua by shuttle or chicken bus, this market will be unlike any market you have ever seen before. English, if spoken at all, is mainly market phrases, with everyone trying to get the most reasonable price.

The market is full of everything you could possibly imagine. There is hot food, organic produce, meat, fish, clothing, shoes, everyday household items and hundreds of handmade artisan gifts. The vendors tend to be entire families - and Mayan families do not come in short supply - so prepare to see people of all ages haggling and bartering throughout the stalls.

Chichicastenango is the perfect place if you're looking to spend some money, especially if you're passionate about supporting local communities. However, even if you don't have a spare dollar to spend, it is more than worth going just for the experience - it is unlikely you will ever find another like it.

48. Get Out of Antigua - Guatemala City

Guatemala City, or 'Guate' as it is more commonly known, is - like Antigua- unlike anywhere else in the country, although in all the opposite ways. Travelers are usually cautioned away from city as its reputation is less than desirable, however, if you enjoy being thrown out of your comfort zone, it is a fascinating and unforgettable place. There are many hostels and hotels that are very tourist friendly, serving as a good base for exploring all the city has to offer. Of course, some of the Zones (or Zonas), are still strict no-go areas, but others are home to wonderful museums, galleries, bars, cafes and restaurants.

Guate is the hub of the country, this is where you will learn the most about Guatemalan culture and see Guatemala in its most raw and authentic state. Huge corporate sky scrapers loom over small shanty towns, making it look like something from a futuristic movie-world. As well as usual city landmarks, there are also ancient Mayan ruins that are largely unexplored by tourists, adding more to the mystery and magic. The city is currently re-inventing itself as a safe and welcoming destination. Taking the time to explore its hidden delights now before it is another tourist hotspot is highly advisable! 49. Get Out of Antigua - Mayan Ruins

The ruins that most tourists will visit are the ruins of Tikel, based in Flores in the north of the country. However, there are also some less-explored ruins a short drive from Antigua, that are lesser-known but almost as impressive.

Iximché

The old capital of the Kaqchikel Mayan Kingdom and now a delightful day trip out from Antigua for when the city starts to feel small and contained. Although the site is a lot smaller than Tikal, it is well-maintained and has an interesting and fruitful history. You can either pay a local and well-informed guide to take you around the ruins, or do some exploring yourself. On site you will also find a small museum and a picnic area for lunch, so remember to pack some avocado and tortillas for a snack!

50. Staying Safe

Although Guatemala is a country of charm and outstanding natural beauty, it certainly has its limitations when it comes to safety. The reality is you have to be aware, especially at night, and moving between cities.

Antigua has a reputation of being on of the safest cities in Guatemala, but there is still an element of danger. The most common type of crime here is petty crime, usually pickpocketing. The pickpockets are not discrete about their profession either, they will happily drive their moped on to the curb and take your phone straight out of your hand, or slash your back pack behind you. Muggings are also common in Antigua, and usually happen between the hours of 10pm-3am. The victims are almost always tourists who underestimate the danger of walking the streets alone at night.

These are a few tips I found the most helpful:

- Separate your cash into different bags

- Have multiple photocopies of your bankcard and passport on you in different places

- Write down the emergency number to call when you have lost your bank card and have it on you at all times

- Do not leave your drink unattended, and be wary when accepting a drink from a stranger

- Do not walk around alone late at night

Most of all, don't let fear stop you from enjoying your travels. Immerse yourself in all this vibrant city has to offer, but do it with awareness and humbleness, as if you were a guest in someone else's house.

> TOURIST

GREATER THAN A TOURIST

Visit GreaterThanATourist.com
http://GreaterThanATourist.com

Sign up for the Greater Than a Tourist Newsletter
http://eepurl.com/cxspyf

Follow us on Facebook:
https://www.facebook.com/GreaterThanATourist

Follow us on Pinterest:
http://pinterest.com/GreaterThanATourist

Follow us on Instagram:
http://Instagram.com/GreaterThanATourist

Rachael Haylock

> TOURIST

GREATER THAN A TOURIST

Please leave your honest review of this book on Amazon and Goodreads. Thank you.

We appreciate your positive and negative feedback as we try to provide tourist guidance in their next trip from a local.

Our Story

Traveling is a passion of the "Greater than a Tourist" series creator. Lisa studied abroad in college, and for their honeymoon Lisa and her husband toured Europe. During her travels to Malta, an older man tried to give her some advice based on his own experience living on the island since he was a young boy. She was not sure if she should talk to the stranger but was interested in his advice. When traveling to some places she was wary to talk to locals because she was afraid that they weren't being genuine. Through her travels, Lisa learned how much locals had to share with tourists. Lisa created the "Greater Than a Tourist" book series to help connect people with locals. A topic that locals are very passionate about sharing.

Rachael Haylock

Notes

Made in the USA
San Bernardino, CA
07 April 2019